SUCCESSFUL AMERICANS

Mexican Americans

Hal Marcovitz

A GALLUP RESOURCE BOOK

Mason Crest Publishers
Philadelphia

Produced by OTTN Publishing in association with
Bow Publications, Inc.

MASON CREST PUBLISHERS INC.
370 Reed Road
Broomall, Pennsylvania 19008
(866) MCP-BOOK (toll free)
www.masoncrest.com

Printed in the United States of America.

First Printing

9 8 7 6 5 4 3 2 1

Library of Congress Cataloging-in-Publication Data

Marcovitz, Hal.
  Mexican Americans / Hal Marcovitz.
     p. cm. — (Successful Americans)
  Includes bibliographical references.
  ISBN-13: 978-1-4222-0515-0 (hardcover)
  ISBN-13: 978-1-4222-0865-6 (pbk.)
  1. Mexican Americans—Juvenile literature. 2. Mexican Americans—Biography—
Juvenile literature. 3. Mexican Americans—Social conditions—Juvenile literature.
I. Title.
  E184.M5M3564 2008
  973'.046872—dc22
                                                              2008029813

Publisher's note:
All quotations in this book come from original sources, and contain the spelling
and grammatical inconsistencies of the original text.

◀ **CROSS-CURRENTS** ▶

When you see this logo, turn
to the Cross-Currents section
at the back of the book. The
Cross-Currents features explore
connections between people,
places, events, and ideas.

Table of Contents

CHAPTER 1   The Mexican-American Experience   5

CHAPTER 2   Pat Mora: Storyteller   12

CHAPTER 3   Bill Richardson: Governor and Diplomat   17

CHAPTER 4   Moctesuma Esparza: Film Producer   23

CHAPTER 5   Antonio Villaraigosa: Politician   29

CHAPTER 6   Salma Hayek: Actress and Activist   34

CHAPTER 7   Los Lonely Boys: Tex-Mex Rock Group   39

CHAPTER 8   Tony Romo: Cowboys Quarterback   44

CROSS-CURRENTS   50

NOTES   56

GLOSSARY   58

FURTHER READING   59

INTERNET RESOURCES   59

OTHER SUCCESSFUL MEXICAN AMERICANS   60

INDEX   62

A mariachi band performs traditional Mexican music at a May 2006 immigration rally in Los Angeles, California. According to some estimates, more than half of illegal immigrants are of Mexican descent.

CHAPTER ONE

The Mexican-American Experience

According to the U.S. Census, about 12 million people living in the United States today were born in Mexico. But many more people of Mexican descent live in country, according to the American Community Survey. It reported in 2006 that 28.3 million people—about 9 percent of the population of the United States—is of Mexican descent. Mexican Americans are the largest Hispanic group in the United States.

FLEEING WAR AND POVERTY

In the early 19th century, the country of Mexico controlled vast expanses of territory of North America. In 1836 one of these regions became the Republic of Texas. It was later annexed by the United States. Conflict over who controlled Texas led to the Mexican-American War.

The war ended in 1848 with the signing of the Treaty of Guadalupe-Hidalgo. The United States acquired from Mexico a vast swath of territory that eventually became parts of Texas as well as California, Colorado, Arizona, New Mexico, Utah, and Nevada. At the same time, tens of thousands of Mexicans who lived in the former Mexican territory suddenly became U.S. citizens.

By the late 1800s much of the wealth of Mexico was under the control of an elite few; the majority of the population lived in terrible poverty. The desire to make a better life for themselves led many Mexicans living south of the U.S.-Mexican border to immigrate north.

HISPANIC AMERICANS

Hispanic Americans are U.S. citizens who can trace their roots back to Mexico, Spain, and the Spanish-speaking nations of South America, Central America, and the Caribbean. The U.S. Census Bureau estimates that Hispanics account for 15 percent of the total population in the United States. By the year 2050, that number is expected to increase to 24 percent.

Still others came to the United States because of civil war. During the early 20th century, the corrupt regime of Mexico's president Porfirio Díaz was challenged by a reform movement led by Francisco Madero. Madero gained in popularity among the Mexican people until Díaz had him arrested and kicked out of the country. That move led to the Mexican Revolution, which began in 1910.

During the next 20 years, as power in Mexico frequently changed hands, approximately 600,000 Mexicans entered the United States. Most were fleeing the violence and unsettled political situation. Others sought refuge from famines and droughts. Many of these Mexican refugees settled in the country and made new lives for themselves.

A NEW LIFE

While a few Mexican immigrants prospered, most scraped by on low-paying jobs. The majority were migrant laborers, traveling to farms where they labored in the fields, picking crops for a few cents a day.

In the 1930s, a period of economic downturn known as the Great Depression caused widespread unemployment, crop failures on farms, factory shutdowns, and other economic problems. Jobs became scarce. Out-of-work Americans took the low-paying jobs traditionally held by Mexican immigrants. To make more jobs available for U.S. citizens, immigration officials cracked down illegal aliens—immigrants who had entered the country without U.S. government permission. Mexicans were rounded up and deported back to Mexico. During this period it is estimated that hundreds of thousands of Mexicans were sent back to their homeland against their will.

Covering around 760,000 square miles (about 2 million sq km), Mexico is comprised of 31 states and the federal district of Mexico City.

Not everyone was deported. Some Mexicans found their way to the camps established by the Depression-era U.S. Farm Security Administration. This government agency set up housing and provided food, housing, medical care, and farm jobs to migrant workers, many of whom were Mexican immigrants.

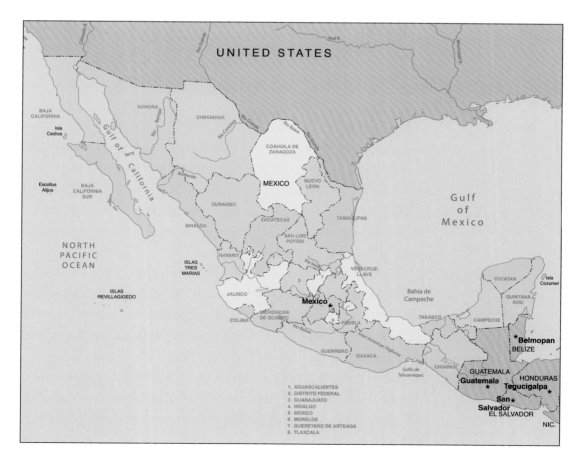

The Mexican-American Experience

Boys living in a Robston, Texas, labor camp in 1942. During the 1930s and 1940s the Farm Security Administration (FSA) established camps to provide housing for migrant farm workers, most of whom were Mexican immigrants.

BRACEROS

During World War II (1939–1945) there were low-paying jobs available again in rural areas. In fact, farmers were desperate for low-cost laborers to pick their crops. The ongoing war caused a labor shortage in America, so farmers asked Congress to establish a guest worker program that would enable Mexicans to work in the United States.

In 1942 Congress adopted the *bracero* program. The term comes from the Spanish word *brazo*, meaning "arm." The program allowed Mexicans to cross the border to work as contract laborers. From 1942 to 1964, when Congress finally repealed the program, an estimated 5 million Mexicans worked as *braceros*.

Some bracero workers moved on to better-paying or nonagricultural jobs in urban areas. They settled in Mexican communities, or barrios, that sprang up in western and southwestern cities such as Los Angeles, California, and El Paso and San Antonio,

Texas. Others traveled farther north, to factory jobs in urban areas such as Detroit, Michigan, and Chicago, Illinois.

Many Mexican immigrants became naturalized citizens, and their U.S.-born children were citizens by birth. They started businesses, graduated from colleges, entered the trades and professions, and become politically active.

DEALING WITH DISCRIMINATION

Throughout the 20th century Mexican immigrants living in the United States encountered discrimination in many areas of life. Some with U.S. citizenship were prevented from voting. Discrimination and racism limited job and educational opportunities.

During the 1950s and 1960s activists began working to achieve rights for migrant workers, improve education, and ensure voting and political rights of Mexican Americans. Their effort became known as the Chicano movement. (The word *Chicano* was used by Mexican activists to proudly identify themselves as Mexican American.)

Mexican farm workers would eventually form the backbone of the American farm labor movement, which developed and grew during the 1950s and 1960s. The United Farm Workers, a union headed by a charismatic leader named Cesar Chavez, helped win higher wages, health care, and other benefits for farm laborers.

ILLEGAL IMMIGRATION

In addition to the 12 million Mexican-born residents legally in the United States today, an estimated 6.2 million Mexicans are believed to be in the country illegally, according to a 2005 report by the Pew Hispanic Center. Some crossed the border illegally by traveling through the desert or by hiding in vans and trucks. Some entered the United States legally but remained beyond the time their visa allowed them to stay.

The Mexican-American Experience

In a 2007 poll conducted by the Gallup Organization, Americans were asked what the higher priority should be in dealing with the issue of illegal immigration. The majority said the U.S. government should halt the flow *and* develop a plan to deal with illegal immigrants living in the United States. In a separate poll taken the same year, 59 percent of the respondents said they favor providing illegal immigrants with a path to citizenship.

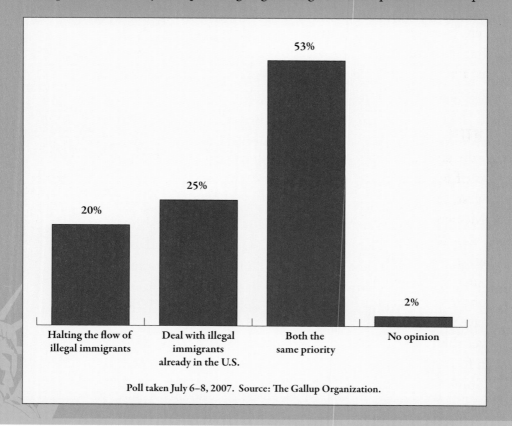

53%

25%

20%

2%

| Halting the flow of illegal immigrants | Deal with illegal immigrants already in the U.S. | Both the same priority | No opinion |

Poll taken July 6–8, 2007. Source: The Gallup Organization.

Illegal immigrants are drawn to the United States by economic opportunity and the chance to obtain a better quality of life. Many take low-wage jobs as restaurant workers, janitors, gardeners, construction workers, or other manual laborers.

Although the positions are low-paid, they allow workers to earn more than they could get if they remained in Mexico. Often money earned in the United States is sent back to families in Mexico. This money, called remittances, has become an essential part of Mexico's economy.

U.S. legislators have been unable to come to a consensus over what to do about illegal immigrants already living in the country. Some politicians believe illegal immigrants should be deported back to Mexico. Others support strong enforcement of current laws but a path to citizenship—giving immigrants already in the country guest worker visas and a chance to become citizens after they prove themselves eligible by holding jobs, paying taxes, and abiding by American laws.

COMMUNITIES

Today, the states with the largest concentrations of Mexican Americans are in the Southwest, and include California, Texas, New Mexico, Arizona, and Nevada. Illinois and Florida also have significant populations. Since the 1970s Midwestern states such as Kansas and Illinois, which offer jobs in meatpacking, agricultural, and other related industries, have also attracted many Mexican immigrants.

Over the years the Mexican culture has influenced U.S. society in foods, language, music, entertainment, and many other areas. Some of the people of Mexican descent who have made significant contributions in music, literature, politics, and sports are featured in the following biographies.

◄ CROSS-CURRENTS ►

To learn more about Americans' opinions on overall immigration to the United States, turn to page 50.

The Mexican-American Experience

CHAPTER TWO

Pat Mora: Storyteller

As Pat Mora was growing up in a comfortable, middle-class home in El Paso, Texas, she was aware that just a few miles away, in the neighboring city of Ciudad Juárez across the Rio Grande, some people in Mexico were living a different kind of life. In the Mexican border town of Ciudad Juárez there were poor neighborhoods in which residents had no electric lights and few other modern conveniences.

The experience of living on the border—not only between two countries but also between two cultures—would be a common theme of many of Mora's stories. This granddaughter of Mexican immigrants would author more than 30 children's books and volumes of poetry in which she explored the Mexican-American experience. She explains, "I am a child of the border, that land corridor bordered by two countries that have most influenced my perception of reality."

Many of Mora's stories also focus on Mexican-American families and on the challenges that young Chicanos face as they grow up in the United States. Some of the characters stumble at first, but they all learn valuable lessons. They are typically aided by mothers, fathers, uncles, aunts, grandparents, or other family members who help them connect with their Mexican roots.

Mora fills some of her stories with the culture, folktales, and people of Mexico—a heritage that she did not truly discover for herself until her adult years. Mora explains, "When I finally realized that I had a sort of vein of gold that I had never tapped, it was like opening that treasure chest. My whole Mexican heritage was something that I could write about."

MEXICAN HERITAGE

Patricia Estella Mora was born January 19, 1942, in El Paso, to Raúl and Estela Mora. Raúl "Roy" Antonio Mora was three years old when he arrived in El Paso. His parents crossed the Rio Grande in 1915, refugees from the violence of the Mexican Revolution. Estela's parents had also fled the revolution in Mexico. Their daughter—Pat's mother—was born and raised in El Paso.

In their bilingual home Raúl and Estela raised three daughters—Pat, Cecilia, and Stella—and a son, Roy Antonio. Pat says she does not recall any time when she did not

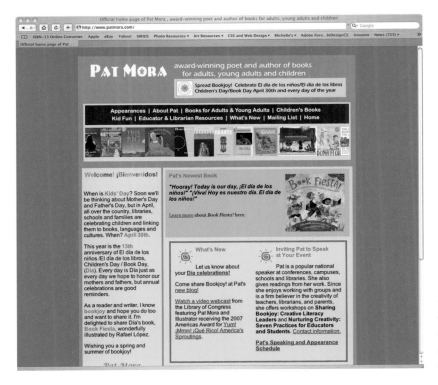

Pat Mora shares her Mexican-American heritage through her children's books and poetry.

know how to speak English or Spanish. The Mora children were exposed to the Mexican culture; Pat's parents and other relatives spoke Spanish and played traditional Mexican music on the radio. At school, though, the language was English and the subjects taught reflected American culture.

Pat attended Catholic schools in El Paso. Even though the city had a large population of Mexican Americans, the nuns who taught class rarely touched on the history or language of the Mexican people. Years later, Mora would tell an interviewer:

> There were times when I wished that my Mexican heritage were a part of my school day. I wished that we had had books that had Spanish in them. And I wished that I had seen things about Mexican culture on the bulletin boards and in the library. One of the reasons that I write children's books is because I want Mexican culture and Mexican-American culture to be a part of our schools and libraries.

A view of a state park in El Paso, near where Mora grew up. A common theme of her books is the desert, which she describes as "open spaces, wide sky, all that sun and all those animals that scurry across the hot sand or fly high over the mountains."

BECOMING A WRITER

In 1960 Mora graduated from high school. She enrolled in Texas Western College in El Paso (known today as the University of Texas-El Paso), where she planned to study medicine. She later changed her major and in the spring of 1963 graduated with a bachelor's degree in English.

That July Pat married her boyfriend, William H. Burnside. The couple had three children, Wiliam Roy, Elizabeth Anne, and Cecilia Anne. Mora worked as a teacher in El Paso and earned a master's degree in English from the University of Texas.

During the 1970s, as Pat raised her children, she worked part-time at a local community college. She also wrote poetry and stories. In 1983 she published her first poem in a Latino anthology for children. The following year she published her first book, *Chants,* a book of poetry. In 1987 Mora produced a second volume of poetry, *Borders.* The poetry in each book recounts the struggles that Chicanos often endure as they try to fit in with American society.

During the 1980s Mora divorced her husband, and married Vernon Lee Scarborough, a college professor. In 1989 the couple moved to Cincinnati, Ohio, where Scarborough had accepted a teaching job. At this point in her life, Mora decided to become a full-time writer.

Three years later, Pat Mora published her first storybook for children. Called *A Birthday Basket for Tía,* the picture book tells the story of how a young girl, Cecilia, finds the perfect present for her *tía,* which is Spanish for aunt. Mora based the character of Cecilia's *tía* on her own aunt, Ignacia Delgado Manquera, who lived with the Mora family when Pat was growing up. The children called Ignacia "Aunt Lobo," which means wolf in Spanish. She acquired the nickname, says Mora, because she referred lovingly to her nieces and nephew as her "little wolves." Mora explains, "I learned the power of storytelling from my aunt. . . . I . . . polish, polish my writing tools to preserve images of women like Lobo, unsung women whose fierce family love deserves our respect."

LATINO LITERATURE

Today, Mora lives in Santa Fe, New Mexico, and she publishes new titles each year. One of her most popular stories is *Tomás and the Library Lady,* which tells the story of the young son of migrant farm workers who discovers the joy of reading. Another well-known title is *Pablo's Tree,* which explores the relationship between a boy and his grandfather, who planted a tree on the day of Pablo's birth. *The Rainbow Tulip* is based on an incident from the childhood of Pat's mother, who as a young girl felt caught between her Spanish home and the outside English-speaking world. The book explores the lessons she learns about herself and her heritage while taking part in the local May Day parade.

◄ **CROSS-CURRENTS** ►

To support literacy in the United States, Pat Mora founded Día. To learn more about this program, turn to page 51.

When she is not writing, Mora is an advocate for children's literacy, an important issue, she says, for all children, including immigrant children growing up in bilingual households. In homes where English is not the primary language it can be hard for a person to learn to read English, Mora says. In 1997 she established *El día de los niños/El día de los libros* (Children's Day/Book Day). Known simply as Día, the annual event, which is now sponsored by the Association for Library Services to Children, is held to encourage reading.

CHAPTER THREE

Bill Richardson: Governor and Diplomat

The son of an American father and Mexican mother, Bill Richardson has spent his life in U.S. politics and public service. He has served as a congressman, delegate to the United Nations (UN), energy secretary, and state governor. A savvy diplomat, Richardson is an expert on foreign policy who has negotiated issues with some of America's most hostile enemies.

TWO WORLDS

Bill Richardson was born on November 15, 1947, in Pasadena, California. His parents, William Blaine Richardson, Jr., and Maria Louisa Lopez-Collada, lived in Mexico City, where William worked as a bank manager. But because William, who was American, wanted his child to have U.S. citizenship, he

The governor of New Mexico, Bill Richardson has also served as a congressman, cabinet official, and ambassador to the United Nations.

sent his Mexican wife to live with his sister in California. Both Bill and his younger sister, Vesta, were born in the United States but spent their childhood in Mexico.

In his autobiography Richardson explains that he was aware that he was a little different from his friends. He lived in two cultures, speaking Spanish with his mother and English with his father. His parents were well-to-do, while many of his friends were born into more modest circumstances. Years later, Richardson recalled,

> When I was growing up, I didn't know whether I was more Mexican or American. Because I hung around with very poor Mexican kids in my neighborhood and played baseball with them . . . but I was also hanging out with some of the kids of my father's friends, who were American. So I was navigating between both of those worlds.

Bill went to primary school in Mexico City. But when he was entering eighth grade he was sent to Middlesex School, an elite boarding school located outside Boston, Massachusetts. Bill was not very fluent in English when he first arrived. Because all the classes were conducted in English, he struggled at first with the academics. He was shy and unsure of himself and had difficulty fitting in.

By his second semester at Middlesex, Richardson was feeling more comfortable with the language. But it was baseball that provided him with some much-needed confidence. He proved to be an outstanding baseball player, and he soon became one of the most popular students on the school's campus. He would later tell an interviewer: "It was baseball that was the bridge for me to be accepted as an American, because I made the varsity that first eighth-grade year."

ENTERING POLITICS

Richardson graduated from Middlesex in 1966. He entered Tufts University in Massachusetts, graduating in 1970. A year later, he was awarded a master of arts degree from Tufts' School of Law and Diplomacy. He spent the next seven years in Washington, D.C., where he worked on the staff for members of the House of Representatives, for the State Department, and for the Senate Foreign Relations Committee.

But Richardson had a goal to be elected to Congress. In 1978 he and his wife, Barbara, moved to New Mexico, where he ran for a seat in the House of Representatives. A Democrat, he sought to represent the First Congressional District, a position held by a longtime Republican incumbent. Richardson lost the 1980 election. Two years later he ran again, this time for a seat representing the newly created Third Congressional District, and he won.

Bill would be reelected seven more times. During his 15 years in the House of Representatives, he sponsored more than a hundred bills. Many became laws. He served on various committees, including the Energy and Commerce Committee, the Interior and Insular Affairs Committee, and the Select Intelligence Committee. He also chaired the Native American Affairs Subcommittee of the Natural Resources Committee.

FOREIGN AFFAIRS AND DIPLOMACY

While in Congress, Richardson gained valuable experience in foreign affairs when President Bill Clinton called on him to aid in the administration's diplomatic efforts. In 1994 Richardson traveled to Haiti to advise the military dictator, Raoul Cédras, to step down or face an American invasion that would restore the island's democratically elected government to power. Two months later, Cédras left office. Later, Richardson negotiated the release of an American pilot whose helicopter had been shot down when it strayed over the North Korean border.

Richardson negotiated with Iraqi leader Saddam Hussein in 1995 to win the release of two Americans from prison.

In the years that followed Richardson was involved in both official and unofficial diplomatic efforts. In 1995 he met with Saddam Hussein, the Iraqi dictator, to negotiate the release of two Americans who had been captured in Iraq after becoming lost in the desert. A year later he met the leader of Cuba, Fidel Castro, to try to negotiate the release of political prisoners. At the year's end he helped win the release of Red Cross workers held hostage in Sudan.

In 1997 Richardson put his diplomatic abilities to use officially. He left Congress that year after receiving a presidential appointment as ambassador to the United Nations. In this position he participated in meetings of the UN General Assembly. He also kept the U.S. State Department informed about what is going on at the international organization.

POLITICAL LEADER

A year later, Clinton named Richardson to his cabinet, appointing him secretary of the Department of Energy (DOE). The DOE deals with the U.S. nuclear weapons program and radioactive waste disposal, as well as with oil and alternative energy issues.

In 2002 Richardson was elected governor of New Mexico. As head of the state, Richardson cut taxes, enforced tough anti-crime laws, worked on developing a statewide water supply plan, and launched initiatives and promoted programs to boost employment and investment in the state. He was reelected in 2006, winning 69 percent of the vote.

While governor of New Mexico, Richardson continued to keep a hand in international diplomacy. In 2007, he met un-officially with President Omar Hassan al-Bashir of Sudan and negotiated a 60-day ceasefire in a rebel conflict that had devastated Sudan's Darfur region.

MAKING A DIFFERENCE

In early 2007 Richardson announced his candidacy for the Democratic Party presidential nomination. His campaign was short-lived. There were numerous Democratic candidates vying for the top position in the race for U.S. president. In both the Iowa caucuses and New Hampshire primary, held in January 2008, Richardson came in fourth. He dropped out of the race soon afterward.

A Korean War veteran shakes Richardson's hand in gratitude during an April 2007 ceremony. The New Mexico governor had successfully negotiated with Korean officials to release the remains of soldiers killed in Korea for final burial in the United States.

In March 2008, after dropping out of the race for the Democratic presidential nomination, Richardson threw his support behind Barack Obama, whose campaign promised change.

After the contest came down to a race between Senators Hillary Rodham Clinton of New York and Barack Obama of Illinois, Richardson endorsed Obama. The New Mexico governor provided the Illinois senator with the support of a key leader in America's politically influential Latino community. Richardson helped bring in the Hispanic vote that ensured Obama's election to the U.S. presidency.

Bill's wife, Barbara, has described her husband as a person constantly seeking solutions. She explains:

> [Bill] has incredible energy; he's driven. He . . . feels very strongly that he can make a difference in people's lives through public service. But he's the kind of person who wants everything done yesterday, and if not, then definitely by the end of the day. He sees everything as a puzzle. If he can't do it one way, he'll do it another.

◄ CROSS-CURRENTS ►

While a Congressman and later as a presidential candidate, Bill Richardson shared his views on the issue of immigration reform. To learn more, turn to page 51.

CHAPTER FOUR

Moctesuma Esparza: Film Producer

As a boy growing up during the 1950s and 1960s in Los Angeles, California, Moctesuma Esparza often went with his father to the movies. Many of the films were Hollywood productions. Others were Spanish-language movie classics in which Mexicans played heroic roles.

When he was older, Moctesuma would become a successful film producer who would look back on his childhood trips to the movies with appreciation: "We'd go to these beautiful movie theaters downtown and see the Mexican art films of the time," he told an interviewer. "I grew up with this beautiful experience of Mexican culture. It was an extraordinary world. . . . I saw 150 movies a year. I had a very full and rich film education as a child."

Los Angeles native and Hollywood producer Moctesuma Esparza has worked to promote the advancement of Latinos in the entertainment industry.

Today, Esparza has established himself as one of the most important Hispanic executives in the U.S. film industry. The films that he has helped create explore Chicano experiences in the United States and retell historical events of America's past.

L.A. NATIVE

Moctesuma was born on March 12, 1949, in East Los Angeles, California, to Francisco and Esther Esparza. They named their son after the Aztec emperor Moctezuma, who ruled Tenochtitlan—today's Mexico City—during the 1500s.

Moctesuma's father was 18 when he immigrated to the United States in 1918, fleeing the fighting of the Mexican Revolution. He settled in Los Angeles, where he eventually found work as a chef in some of the city's most exclusive restaurants. Moctesuma's mother, Esther, died in childbirth when her second son was born.

STUDENT ACTIVIST

Moctesuma attended school in East Los Angeles. During the 1950s and 1960s, schools in the low-income, predominantly Hispanic and black neighborhoods of East L.A. provided few opportunities. As Esparza later recalled, white students in West L.A. were encouraged to study academic courses and prepare for college, while Chicanos were encouraged to enter the trades or find other low-paying jobs. Many students dropped out because of the system, he would later tell an interviewer: "None of us were being programmed to enter college," Esparza explained. "There was a realization that the drop-out rate was not our own failure, but that of the system which programmed us."

Many Chicano students, including Moctesuma, turned to activism to try to improve their educational opportunities. They organized a citywide protest known as the East L.A. walkout, which took place in March 1968. Approximately 20,000 Chicano students from several public high schools participated.

The activists staged marches, demonstrations, and other events throughout the city.

Esparza was among the 13 activists arrested and jailed, charged with disturbing the peace. Crowds rallied to support the leaders, who became known as the East L.A. Thirteen. That response inspired Esparza, he later said, "That was amazing, it was truly amazing. And that gave us tremendous strength to know that the community had come out and decided that, no, they were not going to have their children treated that way and they were not going to have their leadership destroyed."

◀ **CROSS-CURRENTS** ▶

For more information about other Mexican Americans working behind the camera, turn to page 52.

The charges against Esparza and other student activists were eventually dropped. School officials instituted new measures to encourage Chicano students to stay in school, more Mexican-American teachers and administrators were hired, and academic programs such as bilingual education and Chicano studies were put into place.

MAINSTREAM FILMMAKER

When he helped orchestrate the East L.A. walkout, Esparza was a student at the University of California at Los Angeles (UCLA). He had enrolled as a history major, but later switched to studying theatre arts, motion pictures, and television. In many of his student films, he concentrated on making documentaries that focused on political issues.

Esparza graduated from UCLA with a bachelor of arts (1971) and a master of fine arts (1973), both in Theatre Arts-Motion Pictures, TV. As he worked in making commercial theatrical films during the 1980s, he had a goal to portray Hispanics in a positive way, which is something Hollywood did not do. "I decided to create images of human beings—heroes and villains, extraordinary people and ordinary people," he

would later explain. "I would focus on creating positive images of Latinos in film that would destroy the negative stereotypes that came out of Hollywood."

After serving as an executive for a number of well-received films, Esparza coproduced his first major Hollywood production in 1988. *The Milagro Beanfield War*, directed by Hollywood icon Robert Redford, is adapted from a novel about a poor Chicano farmer who takes a stance against greedy developers in Milagro, New Mexico.

By 1993 Esparza had teamed up with screenwriter Robert Katz to form Esparza/Katz Productions, which produced films for television and theater release. One of their ventures was the 1997 film *Selena*, directed by Gregory Nava. It dramatized the life of Tejano music singer Selena Quintanilla Perez, who was murdered in 1995 by a deranged fan. The film starred Jennifer Lopez in a role that helped establish the actress as a major American star.

Although *The Milagro Beanfield War* and *Selena* dramatized events in the lives of Mexican Americans, both films attracted mainstream audiences. In other words, they appealed to audiences both inside and outside the Latino community. Other mainstream films produced by Esparza include the Civil War movies *Gettysburg* (1993) and *Gods and Generals* (2003).

MAYA ENTERTAINMENT

In 2006, nearly 40 years after the citywide demonstrations in Los Angeles, Esparza/Katz Productions released *Walkout*, an HBO film directed by Edward James Olmos. Esparza has said that he wanted to dramatize the event because he had a responsibility to tell younger generations about the struggles of Mexican Americans during the 1960s. He recalled:

> Working on "Walkout" was very dramatic, very emotional for me. I found myself reliving and discovering that there was an immense amount of pain that I had suppressed. In reliving those experiences in the context of my life today, I was able to allow myself to feel and to experience the release of that pain.

A spinoff of Esparza/Katz Productions is Maya Entertainment, a company that produces, distributes, and exhibits films. Esparz founded and runs Maya Entertainment as

A scene from the HBO film Walkout, *which told the story of the 1968 protests by Mexican-American high school students in East Los Angeles.*

Moctesuma Esparza: Film Producer

CEO. A major project is the development of a new theater chain targeted to the Hispanic community. State-of-the-art movie theater complexes, called Maya Cinemas, are being built in U.S. cities across the country to bring to young people the same movie-going experience Esparza had while growing up. The first Maya Cinemas theater opened its doors in Salinas, California, in July 2005.

During his career in the entertainment industry, Esparza has worked to promote the economic advancement of Latinos in the community. He remains hopeful that Latinos will change the Hollywood industry. He says, "We haven't broken in yet. We're in the process, and I expect there to be a huge transformation. . . . Latinos will be an intrinsic part of this industry, and our stories and our heroes will be part of what is produced in a regular basis."

CHAPTER FIVE

Antonio Villaraigosa: Politician

Growing up in a tough inner-city neighborhood, Antonio Villar appeared headed for trouble. Like other young Mexican-American boys in their East Los Angeles barrio, Villar dropped out of school, toyed with the idea of joining a gang, and was quick to settle an argument with his fists. But there were some people in Villar's life who recognized his intelligence and natural leadership abilities. They urged him to return to school. His mother told him, "I just want you to know that I haven't given up on you." Eventually, Villar did return to high school and graduate. He then went on to earn a law degree.

By the 1980s Tony Villar had become Antonio Villaraigosa. He dropped his nickname and in 1987, when he married Corina Raigosa, they combined their surnames. In 2005 Antonio Villaraigosa won the election to become mayor of Los Angeles—becoming the city's first Latino mayor in more than a century. Today, Villaraigosa is one of most politically powerful Hispanic leaders in the United States.

STANDING OUT

Antonio Ramon Villar was born January 23, 1953, in East L.A.'s tough City Terrace community. His father, Antonio Ramon Villar, Sr., emigrated from Mexico to the United States, where he worked as a butcher and cab driver. Tony's mother, Natalia, worked for the California Department of Transportation.

In May 2005 Antonio Villaraigosa was elected mayor of the nation's second-largest city, Los Angeles.

According to Villaraigosa, he and his two sisters, Deborah and Mary Lou, did not have a happy childhood. He has told interviewers that his father was a heavy drinker and abusive husband who beat his wife. When the boy was five years old, Antonio Sr. walked out on the family. His mother remarried four years later.

Villaraigosa was a hardworking student who kept off the streets and excelled in football and track. But during his sophomore year at Cathedral High School, a private all-boys Catholic school in Los Angeles, he was suddenly struck with partial paralysis. Three weeks after doctors operated on a tumor on his spine, Villaraigosa was able to walk again. But he could no longer play sports. He lost interest in his studies, started fighting with other students, and was kicked out of Cathedral High.

Antonio enrolled in the area public high school, Roosevelt High. But he dropped out and spent several months on the streets, getting into trouble. Eventually, he listened to the advice of his mother and Herman Katz, his former English teacher. Katz would later tell reporters why he worked so hard to encourage Villaraigosa to return to school, "It didn't take a genius to figure out there was a lot going on in that head of his. He stood out."

A POLITICAL CAREER

In 1977 Villaraigosa graduated from the University of California at Los Angeles (UCLA) with a degree in history. He later earned a law degree from People's College of Law. However, Villaraigosa did not go on to practice law. Instead, he took a job with the U.S. Equal Employment Opportunity Commission, in which he investigated complaints of prejudice. He later worked as a field organizer for the teachers' union in Los Angeles.

By 1994 Villaraigosa had established himself as one of Los Angeles's most effective political activists. That year, he won his first political election, capturing a seat in the California State Assembly, based in Sacramento. Shortly after the election Corina Villaraigosa filed for divorce, claiming Antonio had been unfaithful. The couple would reconcile, but charges of infidelity would follow him for many years.

Villaraigosa soon earned a reputation as a savvy lawmaker, deft at the art of compromise. He became a protégé of Cruz Bustamante, the powerful speaker of the Assembly. When Bustamante stepped down in 1998, he engineered Villaraigosa's election to succeed him as speaker.

During Villaraigosa's tenure as speaker, the Assembly adopted legislation providing more than $9 billion to build new schools in Los Angeles, as well as $2 billion to expand California's state parks. The Assembly also enacted one of the nation's toughest anti-gun laws during this time. To adopt the legislation, Villaraigosa, who is a Democrat, found it necessary to reach across the aisle and negotiate with Republican lawmakers. He says:

> I'm very much somebody who understands that at the end of the day, you've got to move the ball a little forward. It's not enough to grandstand and protect, you know, your ideological, philosophical spheres of influence and the like, you have to move the ball, and you have to fix problems.

L.A. MAYOR

Villaraigosa made his first run for mayor of Los Angeles in 2001. He lost the election, but gained valuable experience running a citywide campaign. Four years later, he ran against the incumbent Democratic mayor, James K. Hahn.

Racial tensions had surfaced in Los Angeles, and Hahn seemed aloof to these tensions. In fact, he had enraged African-American leaders when he fired Bernard Parks, the city's black police chief. Hahn's administration was also plagued by charges of corruption. As Villaraigosa campaigned in early 2005, he won endorsements from many of the city's African-American political leaders.

In the May elections, Villaraigosa ousted the incumbent mayor, becoming the first Hispanic to be elected mayor of Los Angeles since 1872. Back then, Los Angeles was little more than a dusty frontier crossroads. Today, with nearly 4 million residents, it is the second-largest city in the United States, after New York.

As mayor, Villaraigosa waged an intense campaign to wrest control of the city's schools from the independent Los Angeles Board of Education, which he blamed for the school district's high dropout rate of 30 percent. More programs were needed, he said, to help students whose first language is not English. According to state tests, only 49 percent of students are fluent in English in the school district, Los Angeles Unified.

◀ CROSS-CURRENTS ▶

To see what the Gallup Organization learned when it asked Americans whether fluency in English should be required of immigrants, turn to page 53.

As mayor, Vallaraigosa also boosted the police presence in the city, which led to a dramatic decrease in street crime. In addition, he pushed through the funding of transit projects and backed several renewable energy initiatives designed to reduce L.A.'s energy consumption. For example, in 2008, the city started construction on an 8,000-acre windmill farm that is expected to produce enough energy to supply the needs of 70,000 homes.

In 2007 Corina Villaraigosa again filed for divorce, alleging that her husband had engaged in an affair. Villaraigosa's supporters worried that the scandal would reduce the mayor's standing as a national political figure, but the mayor insisted that he had to follow his heart. In March 2009 the charismatic mayor was reelected to office. His name is among those mentioned as a Democratic Party candidate for California governor sometime in the future.

At a March 2009 event, Villaraigosa appears with California governor Arnold Schwarzenegger.

CHAPTER SIX

Salma Hayek: Actress and Activist

When she was five years old, Hayek sat in a movie theater in her hometown of Coatzacoalcos, Mexico, and watched the film *Willie Wonka and the Chocolate Factory*. It was then that she decided to be an actress and star in movies. The road to Hollywood stardom would include a few twists and turns, but Hayek would eventually realize her dream and establish herself as one of Hollywood's biggest stars. She has also produced and directed numerous critically acclaimed films and television shows.

MEXICAN STARDOM

Salma Valgarma Hayek-Jiménez was born September 2, 1966, in Coatzacoalcos, Mexico. Her father, Lebanese-born Sami Hayek, was an executive for an oil company. Her mother, Diana Jiménez, had been an opera singer. The family was well off, spending winters in the ski resort of Vail, Colorado, and summers touring Europe.

By the age of nine, Hayek had discovered gymnastics and was soon recognized as one of Mexico's most promising young athletes. She trained hard with the goal of eventually joining Mexico's Olympic team. But her father stepped in and decided he did not want his daughter growing up under such pressure. Hayek would later recall, "He said, 'I'm not going to take away the opportunity of my daughter to have a childhood.'" That's when the Hayeks decided to send their daughter to boarding school in the United States.

Salma attended the Academy of the Sacred Heart, an exclusive girls' school in Grand Coteau, Louisiana. The young girl found life in the Catholic boarding school dull and began playing pranks. One of her favorite jokes was setting the clocks back by three hours so the nuns who taught classes would be late. After several incidents, Hayek was booted out of school. Her parents enrolled her at other schools, but she cut classes and continued playing pranks. Salma was eventually brought home to finish school in Mexico City's Universidad Iberoamericana.

But Hayek soon dropped out to pursue an acting career. In 1989 she landed the title role in the Mexican soap opera *Teresa*. The show became an enormous hit and propelled Salma to stardom in Mexico. Two years later, in 1991, she abruptly left the cast and headed off to Hollywood, where she intended to break into American movies.

Born in Mexico, actress and film director Salma Hayek became a U.S. citizen in 2004.

FLOODED WITH OFFERS

Hayek had a rocky start in Hollywood. She landed only minor roles, and struggled with the fact that roles for Hispanics were usually negative ethnic stereotypes: Men were cast as thugs and gang members, while females were maids, prostitutes, or drug addicts. Her first role was in the short-lived American TV series *Street Justice*. She told a reporter: "I played the bride of a gang member, a world I knew nothing about. That was typecasting. I had never even seen a gang member. We don't have them in Mexico, not in my neighborhood."

Salma Hayek: Actress and Activist

Hayek and Antonio Banderas in a scene from the 1995 crime thiller Desperado.

Similar roles followed. But in 1992 Hayek appeared as a guest on a Spanish-language interview show and caught the eye of director Robert Rodriguez. He cast her in a starring role in the action film *Desperado*, opposite Spanish star Antonio Banderas. After the movie was released in 1995, Hayek received a flood of offers to appear in a variety of films. Soon, she was cast alongside such stars as George Clooney, Matthew Perry, Russell Crowe, Matt Damon, and Will Smith.

By the late 1990s, Hayek had established her own production company so that she could have more control over her films. At that time she began work on the film *Frida*, a biography of the tragic Mexican artist Frida Kahlo. In addition to starring in the film, Hayek served as coproducer. Released in 2002 *Frida* received widespread critical acclaim. For her role, Hayek received an Academy Award nomination for Best Actress, making her the Mexican to be nominated for an Oscar.

◀ CROSS-CURRENTS ▶

Hayek was nominated for an Academy Award for the film in which she played Mexican painter Frida Kahlo. To learn more about Kahlo, turn to page 52.

PRODUCER AND DIRECTOR

As a Hollywood star, Hayek was frequently the subject of tabloid gossip columns. Over the years, she was linked romantically to actors Edward Norton and Josh Brolin. She later became engaged to French businessman François-Henri Pinault. In September 2007 their daughter, Valentina Paloma, was born. Hayek and Pinault were married in February 2009 in Paris.

A naturalized American citizen since 2004, Hayek is also a political activist. She has spoken out against domestic violence, even testifying before Congress in 2005. At that time, she called on lawmakers to reauthorize the U.S. Violence Against Women Act. She has helped raise money for the National Domestic Violence Hotline so that the agency can employ bilingual women to take calls from battered Hispanic victims who need help. She says,

Hayek appears at a UNICEF One Pack = One Vaccine event in February 2009. She serves as spokesperson for the campaign, which raises funds to provide tetanus vaccines to mothers and their babies in developing countries.

> Domestic violence is a very important issue to me. I don't feel right even calling it domestic violence. I don't see it as a domestic issue; I see it as a women's rights issue. The way that women have been devalued throughout history is very disturbing. . . . I demand more respect for who we are.

While Hayek looks for new roles, she has also worked behind the camera as a film and TV executive. In 2004, she won a Daytime Emmy Award for Outstanding Directing in a Children/Youth/Family Special for the Showtime TV movie *The Maldonado Miracle*. Hayek also serves as executive producer of the award-winning television series *Ugly Betty*. The show, which premiered on ABC in September 2006, stars America Ferrera. She plays an awkward young Hispanic woman who works as the personal assistant of a high-powered fashion magazine editor. Hayek explains why she likes the character:

> What I love about Betty is that she is a fighter, she has a sense of humor about herself, and she's more confident than anyone else around her. And in a country like ours, the U.S., which is so image-oriented, I wanted to see a show like that on television.

In 2007 *Ugly Betty* was nominated for several Emmys, including Outstanding Comedy Series in 2007. The same year Hayek, who had a guest appearance on the show, was nominated for Outstanding Guest Actress in a Comedy Series.

CHAPTER SEVEN

Los Lonely Boys: Tex-Mex Rock Group

When brothers Henry, Jojo, and Ringo Garza decided to form a band and tour on their own, they easily came up with a name for their group: Los Lonely Boys. After spending years touring as backup musicians for their father—*conjunto* singer Enrique Garza—the Garza boys knew how lonely life could be while on the road. As it turned out, they would attract audiences large enough to keep the group from feeling too lonely.

Fans were drawn to the mix of rock, blues, Mexican, and country music that is the sound of the Los Lonely Boys. "It's complicated [to explain] what we call Texican rock 'n' roll, our music," Jojo says. "Basically it mixes melodies and beats of songs we've heard throughout the years."

CONJUNTO BAND

The three Garzas brothers were born to Mary Ellen and Enrique "Ringo" Garza in San Angelo, a town in central Texas. Henry was born in 1978, Joe Jojo in 1980, and Ringo in 1981.

The town of San Angelo is where the boys' father led his five brothers and sister in a family conjunto band they called Los Falcones. Conjunto is a style of music popular along both sides of the U.S.-Mexican border; it is lively, festive music in which the bass guitar and accordion are the main instruments. Enrique played the *bajo sexton*—a 12-string guitar. During the 1970s and 1980s Los Falcones performed regularly at venues in the border towns of

The three Garza brothers who make up Los Lonely Boys (from left to right, Ringo, Jojo, and Henry) describe their music as Texican rock 'n' roll.

Texas and elsewhere in the Southwest. However, the band fell short of success.

Enrique also held down full-time jobs, mostly in factories or as a truck driver. But he made sure music was part of his boys' lives. Henry took up the guitar and harmonica. Jojo learned the bass guitar as well as keyboards. Ringo learned the drums. The boys were exposed to different genres of music—rock 'n' roll and country as well as Enrique's conjunto sound. "That's where we think our dad was ahead of his time," says Jojo. "He was mixing cultures, putting new things in there."

In 1990 Mary Ellen and Enrique Garza divorced. Mary Ellen took their two daughters to live with her, while Enrique kept the boys. He moved them to Nashville, Tennessee, the country music capital of the United States. Using the boys as his backup musicians, Enrique planned to make it as a solo artist in Nashville. The band played in bars for modest paychecks, usually no more than a few hundred dollars. Enrique later commented on how young his sons were at the time: "People couldn't see Ringo sitting behind the drums. But when [the boys] played, they sounded like adults."

LOS LONELY BOYS

In 1996, the boys decided to split with their father—a band breakup that Enrique encouraged. The following year the musicians released *Los Lonely Boys* on a small label, Sofaking Records. The album received little notice.

A few years later, after the Garza brothers had moved back to Texas, country icon Willie Nelson heard the CD. He had the band re-record their album at his recording studio in Austin. He sat in to provide guidance and he provided some of the vocals on the album. Enrique Garza also contributed to the recording.

Released in 2004 by Epic Records, *Los Lonely Boys* was an instant hit, selling more than 2 million copies. The Garzas became stars. They went on to perform with numerous top acts, including the Rolling Stones, ZZ Top, Tim McGraw, and Carlos Santana. "We went wild," Jojo recalled of those first few months after the re-release of *Los Lonely Boys*. "We went across the country, over to Europe for a while, to the Grammys. It's a big ride, and we feel blessed to meet these people and spread our message."

The visit to the Grammy Award ceremony in February 2005 brought Los Lonely Boys further recognition. Their song "Heaven," from the *Los Lonely Boys* album, won the Garzas a 2005 Grammy Award for Best Pop Performance by a Duo or Group.

ANOTHER PART OF AMERICA

After the success of *Los Lonely Boys*, the Garzas released several follow-up albums of original songs. *Sacred* came out in 2006, and *Forgiven* was released in 2008. The group also produced a holiday album entitled *Christmas Spirit* and some live-performance albums.

Los Lonely Boys took home a Grammy Award in 2005 for their single "Heaven."

Henry Garza plays guitar, Ringo Garza is on drums, and Jojo Garza plays bass guitar for Los Lonely Boys.

The story of Los Lonely Boys and their Texican music was featured in a documentary film called *Cottonfields and Cross-roads*, which was released in 2007. The film was produced by filmmaker Héctor Gálon, who approached the Garzas as they were starting to find an audience for their music. Henry explains, "We really didn't know he was making a documentary or even what it was going to be like, but it was an honor and a blessing to show the rest of the world a Chicano musical family, another part of America."

◀ **CROSS-CURRENTS** ▶

The Garza brothers have toured with another Mexican-American band that inspired the brothers when they were young. To learn more, turn to page 54.

CHAPTER EIGHT

Tony Romo: Cowboys Quarterback

As a young boy growing up in Burlington, Wisconsin, Tony Romo did not consider football his favorite sport. His mother worked at a local golf course, and he spent a lot of time playing golf. A natural athlete, Romo also excelled at basketball and soccer. It was not until his sophomore year at high school that he went out for football, and he was not star player. "You know those guys who throw a nice, tight spiral in high school?" Romo recalls. "That wasn't me."

Eventually, Romo's technique would improve. And his natural athletic ability, leadership skills, and intelligence would help him develop into one of the top quarterbacks in the National Football League (NFL). After taking over as signal-caller for the Dallas Cowboys in 2006, he would help resuscitate a team in need of a talented quarterback. Veteran Cowboys lineman Marco Rivera says of Romo: "This kid is for real. He can take charge in the huddle. He can lead the team. He can play."

A NATURAL ATHLETE

Antonio "Tony" Ramiro Romo was born April 21, 1980, in San Diego, California. His father, Ramiro Romo, Jr., is the son of a Mexican immigrant, and his mother, Joan Romo, is Polish-German. Tony was their third child—joining four-year old Danielle and two-year-old Jossalyn. At the time of Tony's birth, Ramiro was serving in the U.S. Navy. Two years later the family moved to Burlington, Wisconsin.

Tony grew up playing many different sports. He played Little League baseball and started for the Burlington High School basketball team. During his sophomore year in high school he went out for and made the football team but did not get any playing time. A year later, Tony started at quarterback and led the team to a winning season. But the Burlington Demons had a disappointing season of 3 wins and 6 losses during his senior year.

Tony won a partial football scholarship at Eastern Illinois University, in Charleston, Illinois. The school is a National Collegiate Athletic Association (NCAA) Division 1-AA school. Having spent just two years as a high school quarterback, Romo did not bring much experience to the Panthers team. His coaches saw potential in him, though, and urged him to work hard. Romo accepted the challenge. "I threw the ball so much that there was no way not to improve," he explained in an interview. "I threw six days a week, lots of hours a day, the whole year. I never stopped."

Tony Romo has been the starting quarterback for the Dallas Cowboys since 2006.

Tony Romo: Cowboys Quarterback

The work paid off. Romo, who was redshirted as a freshman, would quarterback for Eastern Illinois for three years. During his college career he racked up impressive statistics, compiling a passing record of more than 8,200 yards. In 2002, in the fall of his senior year, he led Eastern Illinois to an 8–3 record and the cochampionship of the Ohio Valley Conference. That December, he became the first player in Eastern Illinois history to win the Walter Payton Award, an honor is given to the top player at the NCAA Division 1-AA level.

Romo prepares to throw a pass downfield during an October 2008 game at Texas Stadium in Irving, Texas.

Romo also caught the attention of NFL scouts. But the following spring he was passed over by all the teams during the 2003 NFL draft. Afterward, the Dallas Cowboys signed Romo as a free agent. That summer he reported to training camp in San Antonio.

UNDER PRESSURE

For many years the Cowboys owed their success on the field to talented quarterbacks such as Don Meredith, Roger Staubach, and Troy Aikman. But after Aikman retired in 2000, the Cowboys struggled with finding a replacement. Over the next six years, eight players started at quarterback for the team. Romo was not among them. For his first three years with the Cowboys he sat on the bench.

As he had done in college, Romo worked hard to learn the Cowboys' passing offense and hone his skills as a quarterback. Each day, he would stay late after practice, throwing passes into a net. While he practiced, Romo rolled left or right, often throwing off balance as he imagined the moves he would make to avoid charging defenders. In an interview with the *Sporting News*, he explained:

> The people who are best under pressure are the ones who have done it a million times. That's what you try to do—throw five or six days a week and put yourself in a position where you've practiced that specific throw enough times. If I've done it before, usually I'm better at it.

For three seasons as an NFL quarterback, Romo did not throw a single regular-season pass. Finally, during the fifth game of the 2006 season, Cowboys coach Bill Parcells gave Romo the chance to quarterback. He entered late in the October 15 game against the Houston Texans and completed his two attempted passes, including a touchdown toss in the 34–6 blowout.

The following week, Parcells put Romo in during the second half of the *Monday Night Football* game against the New York Giants. The Cowboys lost the game, but the coach saw how the young quarterback was able to spark the offense. Six days later, Parcells gave Romo his first start against the Carolina Panthers. Although the Cowboys fell behind early in the game, Romo rallied the offense and eventually led the team to a 35–14 win. Romo remained the starting quarterback for the rest of the season.

NATIONAL CELEBRITY

Romo ended up leading Dallas to the National Football Conference wild card game against the Seattle Seahawks. Late in the fourth quarter of the game, which took place the following January, Dallas was behind by a score of 21–20. But Romo drove his team down the field, putting the Cowboys into the position to win. With a little more than a minute to play, the Cowboys attempted a 19-yard field goal that would give them the game.

When the ball was snapped to Romo, whose job was to hold the ball for the kicker, it slipped through his hands. Although

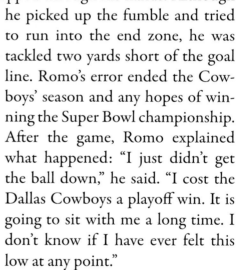

he picked up the fumble and tried to run into the end zone, he was tackled two yards short of the goal line. Romo's error ended the Cowboys' season and any hopes of winning the Super Bowl championship. After the game, Romo explained what happened: "I just didn't get the ball down," he said. "I cost the Dallas Cowboys a playoff win. It is going to sit with me a long time. I don't know if I have ever felt this low at any point."

Romo's teammates and the fans in Dallas have forgiven him. Since the botched field goal, he has led the Dallas Cowboys to some very successful seasons. Romo has energized fans and at the same time become a national celebrity. He has

As kicker Martin Gramatica attempts a field goal against the Seattle Seahawks late in the National Football Conference wild card game on January 6, 2007, Romo mishandles the snap. The Seahawks defeated the Cowboys, 21–20.

even become a pop-culture sensation after being linked romantically to singers Carrie Underwood and actress Sophia Bush. He and Jessica Simpson have dated since 2007.

As a third-generation Mexican American, Tony Romo speaks little Spanish. But he takes pride in his heritage, his grandfather says. When Ramiro Romo, Sr., watched his grandson start for the first time as quarterback for the Cowboys, he told the *San Antonio Express-News:* "I thought of how far we've come, not only as a family, but as a people. I remembered the hard times in Mexico and how I struggled when I first got here. It's like coming from zero to where we are today."

◀ CROSS-CURRENTS ▶

Mexican Americans have competed in professional sports for decades but it was not until 2003 that someone of Mexican descent owned a pro sports team. To learn more, turn to page 55.

ATTITUDES TOWARD IMMIGRATION

The Gallup Organization surveys people around the world to determine public opinion regarding various political, social, and economic issues. One issue that Gallup has researched over the years is immigration to the United States. In general, Americans have a positive view of immigration, reports the Gallup Web site:

> Three in four [Americans] have consistently said it has been good for the United States in the past, and a majority says it is good for the nation today. However, Americans still seem interested in limiting the amount of immigration.

When asked in a July 2008 Gallup survey about the level of immigration into the United States, 39 percent of Americans favored decreasing the number of immigrants allowed into the country, a decrease from 45 percent a year earlier. However, only 18 percent believe it should be increased.

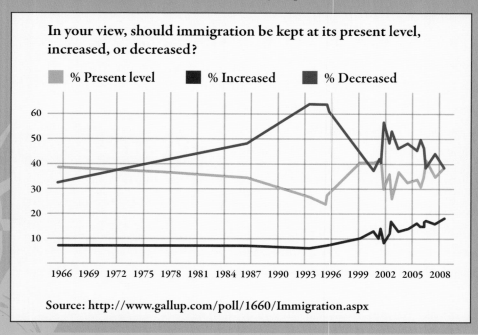

In your view, should immigration be kept at its present level, increased, or decreased?

% Present level   % Increased   % Decreased

Source: http://www.gallup.com/poll/1660/Immigration.aspx

CELEBRATING DÍA

After learning that April 30 is celebrated annually in Mexico as the Day of the Child, Pat Mora worked to extend the tradition to the United States. But she decided to celebrate literacy—the ability to read—for children on that same date. In 1997 librarians in Arizona, New Mexico, and Texas became part of the first effort to celebrate Día (the shortened form of *El día del niño/El día del libro*—Children's Day/Book Day).

Dia has evolved into a cross-cultural celebration of children and reading. It is held annually on or around April 30 in schools and libraries across the United States and in Puerto Rico. Celebrations honor children's home languages and cultures, and promote bilingual and multilingual literacy. Events may include storytelling, talks by children's authors and entertainers, puppet shows, appearances by storybook characters, book giveaways, and music and crafts activities.

Mora has said that she wishes Día was celebrated every day of the year: "I always say it's not just a one-day event. It is the day in which we celebrate all across the country the hard, but joyful, work of a year of linking all children to books, languages and cultures."

BILL RICHARDSON AND IMMIGRATION REFORM

Soon after entering Congress in 1983, Bill Richardson dealt with legislation to reform immigration laws. He supported a bill that would grant legal status to tens of thousands of illegal immigrants already in the country, but also penalize employers who knowingly hired illegal aliens. Richardson's Hispanic colleagues opposed the new bill, believing that it would lead to discrimination by employers against job applicants who looked foreign. Eventually Congress passed and President Ronald Reagan signed the Immigration Reform and Control Act of 1986.

As it turned out, the bill did not reduce the number of illegal immigrants in the United States. Some experts think it has even increased illegal immigration. While still in Mexico or other Latin American countries, many people planning to immigrate to the United States would simply obtain fraudulent documents, such as birth certificates, to use to prove citizenship to prospective employers.

Since becoming governor of New Mexico, Richardson has favored tough border controls to arrest illegal aliens as they enter the country. And he has helped fund the establishment of a fraudulent document task force to root out suppliers of fake documents. Richardson also favors a path to citizenship program for illegal immigrants. He supports providing them with opportunities to become citizens after they prove themselves law-abiding, able to pay taxes, and capable of speaking English.

MEXICAN-AMERICAN FILMMAKERS

Other Mexican Americans who are working behind the camera as writers, producers, and directors include the following:

Gregory Nava (1949–   ): Film director, producer, and screenwriter, Nava was nominated for an Emmy Award for Outstanding Miniseries for *American Family* (2002), and nominated for an Oscar for directing *El Norte* (1983). Nava was the director of *Selena* (1997); screenwriter for *Frida* (2002); and producer, screenwriter, and director of *Bordertown* (2007).

Jesús Salvador Treviño (1946–   ): A director of various episodes of television programs during the 1990s and 2000s, Treviño has worked on *Third Watch* (1999), *Resurrection Blvd.* (2000), *Prison Break* (2005), and many other shows.

Luis Valdez (1940–   ): A playwright, writer, and film director, Valdez is the first Chicano director to have a play performed on Broadway—*Zoot Suit*, in 1979. It tells the story of a group of Mexican Americans wrongfully charged with murder in 1942, and a series of riots that took place the following year in Los Angeles known as the Zoot suit riots. Valdez directed the film version in 1981. He is also known for the Chicano film *I Am Joaquin* (1970) and for the film biography of Ritchie Valens called *La Bamba* (1987).

FRIDA KAHLO

In the 2002 film *Frida*, Salma Hayek plays artist Magdalena Carmen Frida Kahlo. Hayek describes the work of the controversial Mexican painter, saying, "When I first saw her paintings, I didn't necessarily like them. I thought they were so strange and almost shocking, but I couldn't get them off my mind."

Kahlo was born in 1907 in Mexico City to Guillermo and Matilda Kahlo. She had hoped to pursue a career as a physician, but at the age of 15 was severely injured in a bus accident. In the years that followed she would undergo multiple surgeries and live in severe pain because of the accident.

During her convalescence Kahlo took up painting. She would eventually produce 143 paintings, a third of which are self-portraits that mostly explore the pain and sorrows of her life. Her work is based on Mexican folk art, and interweaves fact and fantasy—bizarre or unexpected images are combined with realistic ones. The 1946 painting *The Little Deer*, for example, shows Kahlo's head on the body of a deer that has been shot with arrows. Kahlo died in July 1954 at the age of 47 from complications related to her injuries in the bus accident.

ENGLISH PROFICIENCY

os Angeles Mayor Antonio Villaraigosa grew up in an English-speaking home. Although English was his first language, he learned Spanish so that he could communicate with his Hispanic constituents. The U.S. Department of Education reports that English is a second language to some 10 percent of all American public school students. Their first language is Spanish or an Asian language. Most Americans believe that immigrants should become proficient in English, as the results of the following Gallup poll question show:

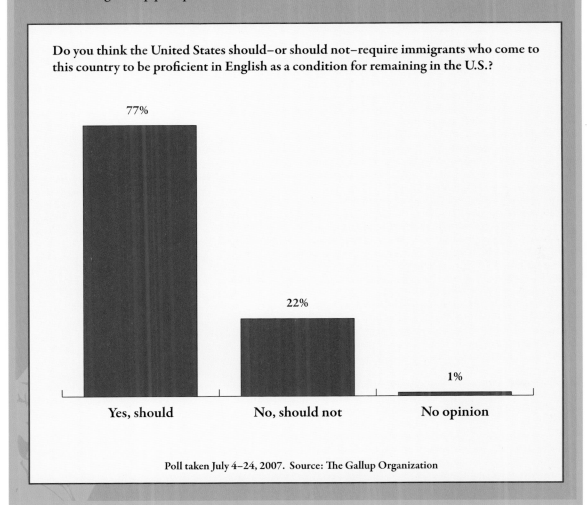

Do you think the United States should–or should not–require immigrants who come to this country to be proficient in English as a condition for remaining in the U.S.?

77%

22%

1%

Yes, should   No, should not   No opinion

Poll taken July 4–24, 2007. Source: The Gallup Organization

LOS LOBS

Jojo Garza of the Los Lonely Boys points to several other Mexican and Mexican-American singers and musicians as inspiration. They include Ritchie Valens, Carlos Santana, and Freddy Fender. Yet another Mexican-American band that helped pave the way for Los Lonely Boys was the three-time Grammy Award–winning group Los Lobos. "Those guys opened the doors for Latin and Hispanic artists," Jojo says. "We're definitely connected through music."

The band, whose name *Los Lobos* is Spanish for "the Wolves" came together in the 1970s in East Los Angeles. Its members have performed together for more than 30 years. One of the band's biggest hits is its version of the traditional song "La Bamba," first popularized in the 1950s by singer Ritchie Valens. Los Lobos released the song in 1987 as part of the soundtrack for a movie about Valens's life. The song hit number 1 on the 1987 Billboard charts.

During the summer of 2008 Los Lonely Boys toured with Los Lobos. "They're living legends to us," JoJo Garza told the *Houston Chronicle*. "We couldn't be more ecstatic about it. It's a real honor to share the stage with them. . . . They did pave the way for a lot of Latin-American artists who sing rock 'n' roll and do traditional stuff, too."

Cesar Rosas (left), Conrad Lozano (center), and Louie Perez of Los Lobos perform at a February 2009 concert.

ARTURO MORENO, PRO SPORTS TEAM OWNER

Mexican Americans have competed in professional sports for decades. But it would not be until 2003 that a Mexican American would own a professional sports team. That year, billionaire Arturo "Arte" Moreno purchased the Anaheim Angels baseball team from the Walt Disney Company.

Moreno, who was born in 1946, earned a degree in marketing from the University of Arizona, in Tucson. After graduating from college in 1973, he took a job as a salesman for a billboard company. It was a modest beginning—his first commission check was just $2.25. Moreno proved to be an enormously successful salesman. Seven years later he was president of Outdoor Systems—another billboard company. He invested in the company and in 1996 Outdoor Systems sold shares to investors on the stock exchange. Two years later, Moreno sold the company for $8 billion.

In 2003, as the new owner of the Angels, Moreno renamed the team the Los Angeles Angels. That move infuriated many fans because the club does not play in Los Angeles, but in the suburb of Anaheim, California. But Moreno wanted people to identify the team with the entire Los Angeles metropolitan area, not one of its suburbs. Fans who complained eventually changed their minds as Moreno helped guide the Angels to some of their most successful seasons.

Arturo Moreno, owner of the Los Angeles Angels of Anaheim.

NOTES

CHAPTER 2

p. 12: "I am a child of the border . . ." Quoted in Scot Peacock, ed., *Contemporary Authors New Revision Series,* Vol. 112. Farmington Hills, Mich.: Thomson Gale, 2003, 235.

p. 12: "When I finally realized that . . ." "Transcript from an Interview with Pat Mora," WETA: Colorín Colorado, 2008. http://www.colorincolorado.org/read/meet/mora/transcript

p. 14: "There were times when I . . ." Quoted in "Teachers: Student Activities: Pat Mora Interview Transcript," Scholastic, 2009–1996. http://teacher.scholastic.com/ACTIVITIES/hispanic/moratscript.htm

p. 14: "open spaces, wide sky . . ." "Pat Mora: Biography," Scholastic: Teachers, http://www2.scholastic.com/browse/contributor.jsp?id=3408

p. 15: "I learned the power of storytelling . . ." Quoted in Peacock, *Contemporary Authors New Revision Series,* Vol. 112*,* 234.

CHAPTER 3

p. 18: "When I was growing up, I didn't know . . ." Quoted in Joel Achenbach, "The Pro-Familia Candidate," *Washington Post*, May 21, 2007, C-1.

p. 18: "It was baseball that . . ." Quoted in Achenbach, "The Pro-Familia Candidate," C-1.

p. 22: "[Bill] has incredible energy . . ." Quoted in Kimberly Swick Slover, "A First Lady for the People: Barbara Flavin Richardson '69" *Colby-Sawyer Alumni Magazine*, Spring/Summer 2005, 13, 17.

CHAPTER 4

p. 23: "We'd go to these beautiful . . ." Quoted in Greg Hernández, "Moctesuma Esparza," *Hispanic*, November 2005, 38.

p. 24: "None of us were being . . ." Quoted in Victor Payan, "Interview with Moctesuma Esparza," *In Motion*, May 21, 1998. http://www.inmotion-magazine.com/mesparza.html

p. 25: "That was amazing, it was . . ." Quoted in "Interview with Moctesuma Esparza," HBO Films. http://www.hbo.com/films/walkout/interviews/esparza.html

p. 25: "I decided to create . . ." Agustin Gurz, "Celluloid Heroes Can Be Latino Too," *Los Angeles Times*, March 11, 2000, B-3. http://articles.latimes.com/2000/mar/11/local/me-7645

p. 27: "Working on *Walkout* was. . ." Quoted in Gabriel de Lerma, "The Advocate of Equality," *Latino Leaders*, August 1, 2006. http://www.latinoleaders.com/articulos.php?id_sec=2&id_art=139

p. 28: We haven't broken in . . ." Quoted in Gabriel de Lerma, "Moctesuma Esparza: The Advocate of Equality," *Latino Leaders*, August 1, 2006. http://www.latinoleaders.com/articulos.php?id_sec=2&id_art=139

CHAPTER 5

p. 29: "I just want you . . ." Quoted in "Antonio Villaraigosa," Clifford Thompson, ed., *Current Biography Yearbook 2007*. New York: H. W. Wilson, 2007, 558.

p. 30: "It didn't take a genius. . ." Quoted in Ira Rifkin, "Making New Friends," *The Jerusalem Report*, June 27, 2005, p. 24.

p. 31: "I'm very much somebody . . ." Quoted in Thompson, editor, *Current Biography Yearbook 2007*, 558.

CHAPTER 6

p. 34: "He said, 'I'm not going to . . .'" Quoted in Robert Sullivan, "Free Spirit," *Vogue*, June 2005. http://www.style.com/vogue/feature/052305/page2.html

p. 35: "I played the bride . . ." Quoted in Sullivan, "Free Spirit."

p. 37: "Domestic violence is . . ." Quoted in Valdes-Rodriguez, "Salma Hayek," *Redbook*, November 2006, 122.

p. 38: "What I love about . . ." Quoted in Valdes-Rodriguez, "Salma Hayek."

CHAPTER 7

p. 39: "It's complicated . . ." David Dorantes, "Los Lonely Boys Plan a Big Night at House of Blues," *Houston Chronicle*, October 29, 2008. http://www.chron.com/disp/story.mpl/ent/6084568.html

p. 40: "That's where we . . ." Quoted in Stewart Oksenhorn, "Lone Stars: Texas-based Los Lonely Boys Seek 'Sacred' Sound," *Aspen Times*, September 3, 2006. http://www.aspentimes.com/article/20060903/109030067

p. 41: "People couldn't see Ringo . . ." Quoted in Edwards, "All in the Family," *Rolling Stone*, September 2, 2004, 72.

p. 41: "We went wild . . ." Quoted in Oksenhorn, "Lone Stars."

p. 43: "We really didn't know . . ." Quoted in Marissa Rodriguez, "Homecoming Kings," *Hispanic*, April 2007, 56.

CHAPTER 8

p. 44: "You know those guys who throw . . ." Quoted in Tim Layden, "Silver Star," *Sports Illustrated*, December 11, 2006, 66.

p. 44: "This kid is for real . . ." Quoted in Layden, "Silver Star."

p. 45: "I threw the ball so much . . ." Quoted in Layden, "Silver Star."

p. 47: "The people who are best under pressure . . ." Quoted in Ryan Fagan, "Star Quality," *Sporting News*, August 13, 2007, 12.

p. 48: "I just didn't get the ball down . . ." Quoted in Jim Corbett, "Magical Season Bobbled Away," *USA Today*, January 8, 2007, C-5.

p. 49: "I thought of how far we've come . . ." Quoted in David Flores, "Romo's Grandparents Revel in His First Game as Cowboys' Starting QB," November 2, 2006, *San Antonio Express-News*. http://www.mysanantonio.com/sports/football/nfl/cowboys/stories/MYSA110306.01D.FBNcowboys.romo.2c1062c.html

CROSS-CURRENTS

p. 50: "Three in four [Americans] have . . ." Quoted in "Immigration," Gallup, 2008. http://www.gallup.com/poll/1660/Immigration.aspx

p. 51: "I always say . . ." "Transcript from an Interview with Pat Mora," WETA: Colorín Colorado, 2008. http://www.colorincolorado.org/read/meet/mora/transcript

p. 52: "When I first . . . " Quoted in Penelope Cruz, "Interview and Portfolio: Salma Hayek," *Interview*, April 2003, 122.

p. 54: "Those guys opened . . ." David Dorantes, "Los Lonely Boys Plan a Big Night at House of Blues," *Houston Chronicle*, October 29, 2008.

http://www.chron.com/disp/story.mpl/ent/6084568.html

p. 54: "They're living legends . . ." John Sinkevics, "Tour with Los Lobos Has Los Lonley Boys Living the Dream," *The Grand Rapids Press*, August 3, 2008. http://www.mlive.com/entertainment/grand-rapids/index.ssf/2008/08/tour_with_los_lobos_has_los_lo.html

GLOSSARY

Academy Award—an annual award of excellence given by the Academy of Motion Picture Arts and Sciences for movie acting and filmmaking; often referred to by its nickname, the Oscar.

cabinet—officials who serve as advisors to the president of the United States; most members of the cabinet head departments charged with overseeing defense, foreign policy, the national treasury, and other agencies of the U.S. government.

Congress—the lawmaking body of the federal government.

dictator—a leader of a government who usually obtains power by force and rules through threats, intimidation, and terror.

documentary—a film that depicts newsworthy events and other contemporary issues in which the actual people involved—not actors—are depicted onscreen.

Emmy Award—an annual top honor presented by the Academy of Television Arts and Sciences for acting, writing, and production in the television industry.

free agent—in sports, a player who is not under contract and is free to join any team.

Grammy—an award given by the National Academy of Recording Arts and Sciences for excellence in the music industry.

label—a company that produces recorded music.

legislation—a proposal drafted by lawmakers that is voted on by members of Congress or state assemblies; if it passes Congress and is approved by the president, it becomes federal law.

naturalized citizen—an immigrant who has become a U.S. citizen; the process of naturalization involves learning English; displaying a knowledge of U.S. history, government, and laws; and swearing an oath of allegiance to the United States.

NFL draft—an annual event conducted by the National Football League in which graduating college players are selected by NFL teams.

quarterback—the football player who directs the team's offensive play; the quarterback executes the play, often by passing the ball to an open receiver.

soap opera—a daily drama, usually told in serial form, aired on TV in the United States and other countries; the name *soap operas* evolved because in the early days of radio, these programs were often sponsored by soap companies.

speaker—the top position in the U.S. House and most state assemblies, the speaker controls the flow of legislation and appoints lawmakers to chair committees.

State Department—the agency of the federal government charged with overseeing U.S. foreign policy.

stereotype—an image, often unfairly conceived, of a person or group of people based on past perceptions of similar people or groups.

FURTHER READING

Dougherty, Terri. *Salma Hayek*. Farmington Hills, Mich.: Lucent Books, 2008.

Engel, Mac. *Tony Romo: America's Next Quarterback*. Chicago: Triumph Books, 2007.

Hernandez, Roger E. *Gallup Major Trends and Events: Immigration*. Broomall, Pa.: Mason Crest Publishers, 2007.

Richardson, Bill. *Between Worlds: The Making of an American Life*. New York: G. P. Putnam's Sons, 2007.

Schroeder, Michael. *The New Immigrants: Mexican Americans*. New York: Chelsea House Publications, 2006.

INTERNET RESOURCES

http://frontiers.loc.gov/learn/features/immig/alt/mexican.html
This Web site maintained by the Library of Congress focuses on the immigration experience of Mexicans. It features a brief history of Mexican immigration and stories about the experiences of Mexican Americans.

http://www.gallup.com
The Gallup Organization provides insights into social issues, politics, sports, the environment, and other facets of life has through the results of polls available on its Web site.

http://www.governor.state.nm.us/index2.php
The official Web site for the New Mexico governor's office includes a biography of Bill Richardson as well as updates on his current activities and positions on issues in his state.

http://www.lacity.org/mayor/
The official Web site of the Los Angeles mayor's office includes a biography of Mayor Antonio Villaraigosa and transcripts of speeches that he has delivered.

http://www.loslonelyboys.org
Fans of Los Lonely Boys can read about Henry, Jojo, and Ringo Garza on the band's official Web site. It includes biographies, the band's touring schedule, and audio files.

http://www.patmora.com
The official Web site of Pat Mora includes brief descriptions of her books.

OTHER SUCCESSFUL MEXICAN AMERICANS

Alexis Bledel (1981–): The daughter of a Mexican mother and Argentine father, Texas-born Bledel is an actress and former model. She has appeared in such films as *Bride and Prejudice* (2004) and *The Sisterhood of the Traveling Pants* (2005). She also starred in the television show *Gilmore Girls* (2000–2007).

Cesar Chavez (1927–1993): As founder of the United Farm Workers of America, Cesar Chavez organized thousands of Latino fruit pickers in California and other western states. Their efforts earned higher wages and health care and other benefits for members. In 1968, Chavez led a nationwide boycott of table grapes when California growers refused to sign labor contracts with his union.

Henry Cisneros (1947–): The grandson of Mexican immigrants, Henry Cisneros was elected mayor of San Antonio, Texas, in 1981. At that time he became the first Mexican American to serve as the town's mayor since 1842. Cisneros held the mayor's seat for four terms, then served in the cabinet of President Bill Clinton as secretary of Housing and Urban Development.

Anthony Nomar Garciaparra (1973–): Third-baseman Anthony Nomar Garciaparra made his Major League debut in 1996 with the Boston Red Sox. He has gone on to play for the Chicago Cubs and Los Angeles Dodgers, earning six trips to the All-Star Game and compiling a lifetime batting average of over .300.

Nancy Lopez (1957–): Nancy Lopez learned to play golf at the age of 8; by the age of 21, she was competing on the Ladies Professional Golf Association (LPGA) tour. In 1978, her first year on the tour, she was named Rookie of the Year, Player of the Year, and Associated Press Female

Ellen Ochoa became the first Hispanic woman in space in April 1993 when she flew aboard space shuttle Discovery *as a mission specialist.*

Athlete of the Year. She has also been inducted into the Golf Hall of Fame.

Ellen Ochoa (1958–): Born in Los Angeles, Ochoa became the first Hispanic woman in space in 1993. An electronic engineer, she served as a mission specialist aboard *Discovery* for that flight. She subsequently returned to space on two more missions.

Edward James Olmos (1947–): Born in Los Angeles, Olmos has acted in the hit TV shows *Miami Vice*, *Battlestar Gallactica*, and *The West Wing*. His films include *Blade Runner* and *Selena* (in which he played the father of the Tejana singer). He was nominated for an Oscar for his role in *Stand and Deliver*, a biography of teacher Jaime Escalante, who worked with disadvantaged East L.A. students.

Eva Longoria Parker (1975–): Born in Corpus Christi, Texas, of Mexican-American parents, Longoria became known as a television actress after appearing in the soap opera *The Young and the Restless* (2001–2003) and *Desperate Housewives* (2004). She also models and holds endorsement contracts with several clothing retailers.

Linda Ronstadt (1946–): Pop singer Linda Ronstadt scored many hits during the 1960s, 1970s, and 1980s, including "Different Drum," "Blue Bayou" and "You're No Good." She has won several Grammy Awards and acted in films.

Carlos Santana (1947–): Guitarist Carlos Santana has been a rock 'n' roll fixture since

United Farm Workers of America president Cesar Chavez.

1969, when he took the stage at the Woodstock rock festival. Since then, Santana has recorded numerous hits and won several Grammy Awards. Santana recorded his biggest hit, "Black Magic Woman," in 1970.

Other Successful Mexican Americans

INDEX

Photo captions are noted in **_bold italic._**

Aikman, Troy, 47
Arizona, 5, 11

Banderas, Antonio, *36*
barrio, 8, 29
al-Bashir, Omar Hassan, 21
A Birthday Basket for Tía (1992 book), 15
Borders (1986 book), 15
Boston, 18
bracero program, 8
Brolin, Josh, 36
Burlington, Wisconsin, 44, 45
Burnside, Cecilia Anne, 15
Burnside, Elizabeth Anne, 15
Burnside, William H., 15
Burnside, William Roy, 15
Bush, Sophia, 49
Bustamante, Cruz, 31

California, 4, 5, 8, 11, 18, 23, 24, 29, 31, 33
Carolina Panthers, 47
Castro, Fidel, 19
Cédras, Raoul, 19
Chants (1984 book), 15
Chavez, Cesar, 9
Chicago, 9
Chicano movement, 9
Cincinnati, 15
Ciudad Juárez, 12
Clinton, Bill, 19, 20
Clinton, Hillary Rodham, 22, *32*
Clooney, George, 36
Coatzacoalcos, 34
Colorado, 5, 34
Congress, 8, 11, 19, 37, 51

Cottonfields and Crossroads (2007 documentary film), 43
Crowe, Russell, 36
Cuba, 20

Dallas Cowboys, 44, *45*, 46, 47–48, 49
Damon, Matt, 36
Darfur, 21
Desperado (1995 film), 36
Detroit, 9
Díaz, Porfirio, 6

East Los Angeles, 24, 25, 29, 54
East L.A. walkout of 1968, 24–25, *27*
Eastern Illinois University, 45, 46
El día de los niños/El día de los libros, 16, 51
El Paso, 8, 12, 13, 14, 15
Esparza, Moctesuma
   activism of, 24–25
   birth and childhood, 23, 24–25
   professional career, 25–28
Esparza/Katz Productions, 26, 27

Farm Security Administration, 7, *8*
Ferrera, America, 37
Forgiven (2008 album), 42
Frida (2002 film), 36, 52

Gallup polls
   attitudes toward immigration, 9, 50
   English proficiency, 53
Gálon, Héctor, 43
Garza, Henry, 39–43
Garza, Jojo, 39–43
Garza, Ringo, 39–43
Garza, Enrique, 39, 40, 41

Garza, Mary Ellen, 39, 41
Gettysburg (1993 film), 27
Gods and Generals (2003 film), 27
Gramatica, Martin, *48*
Great Depression, 6
Guerra, Jackie, *26*

Hahn, James K., 32
Haiti, 19
Hayek, Salma
   birth and childhood, 34–35
   honors received by, 36, 38
   professional career of, 35–36, 38
Hayek, Sami, 34
"Heaven" (2004 single), 42
Houston Texans, 47
Hussein, Saddam, 19

Illinois, 11, 22
Immigration Reform and Control Act of 1986, 51
Iraq, 19

Jiménez, Diana, 34

Kahlo, Frida, 36, 52. *See also Frida* (2002 film)
Kansas, 11
Katz, Herman, 30
Katz, Robert, 26

Lopez, Jennifer, *26*
Lopez-Collada, Maria Louisa, 17
Los Angeles, *4*, 8, 23, 29, 30, 31, 32, 33
Los Angeles Angels of Anaheim, 55
Los Falcones, 39–40
Los Lobos, 54
Los Lonely Boys, 39–43, 54

Los Lonely Boys (1997 album), 41
Los Lonely Boys (2004 album), 41

McGraw, Tim, 41
Madero, Francisco, 6
The Maldonado Miracle (2004 TV movie), 38
Manquera, Ignacio Delgado, 15–16
Marie, Constance, *26*
Maya Entertainment, 27–28
Meredith, Don, 47
Mexican Americans
    discrimination against, 9–11
    experiences and culture, 6–9, 10–11, 12, 13–14, 15, 18, 22, 23, 43
    immigration trends of, *4*, 5–11, 51
    illegal immigration, *4*, 9–11, 51
    population of, 5, 6, 9, 11
Mexican Revolution, 6, 13, 24
Mexico, 5, 6, *7*, 11, 12, 13, 17, 18, 24, 29, 34, 35, 49, 51
Mexico City, 17, 18, 35, 52
Middlesex School, 18
The Milagro Beanfield War (1988 film), 26, 27
Moctezuma (Aztec emperor), 24
Mora, Cecilia, 13
Mora, Estela, 13
Mora, Pat
    birth and childhood, 12–15
    as literary advocate, 16, 51
    stories of, 12, 15–16
Mora, Raúl "Roy" Antonio, 13
Mora, Roy Antonio, 13
Moreno, Arturo, 55

Nashville, 41
Nava, Gregory, 26, 52
Nelson, Willie, 41
Nevada, 5, 11
New Mexico, 5, 11, 16, 19, 21, 51
New York, 22, 33
New York Giants, 47
North Korea, 19

Norton, Edward, 36

Obama, Barack, 22
Olmos, Edward James, *26*, 27

Pablo's Tree (1994 book), 16
Parcells, Bill, 47
Parks, Bernard, 32
Perez, Selena Quintanilla, 26. *See also* Selena (1997 film)
Perry, Matthew, 36
Pew Hispanic Center, 9
Pinault, François-Henri, 36
Pinault, Valentina Paloma, 36
Puerto Rico, 51

The Rainbow Tulip (1999 book), 16
Reagan, Ronald, 51
Redford, Robert, 26
remittances, 11
Richardson, Barbara, 19, 22
Richardson, Bill
    birth and childhood, 17–18
    political career, 17, 19–22, 51
Richardson, William Blaine, 17
Rio Grande, 12, 13
Rivera, Marco, 44
Rodriguez, Robert, 36
Rolling Stones, 41
Romo, Antonio "Tony" Ramiro
    birth and childhood, 44–46
    NFL career of, 46–48
Romo, Danielle, 44
Romo, Joan, 44
Romo, Jossalyn, 44
Romo, Ramiro Jr., 44, 49

San Angelo, 39
San Antonio, 8, 46
Sacramento, 31
Sacred (2006 album), 42
Santa Fe, 16
Santana, Carlos, 41,
Scarborough, Vernon Lee, 15
Schwarzenegger, Arnold, *33*
Seattle Seahawks, 48

Seda, Jon, *26*
Selena (1997 film), 26, 27
Simpson, Jessica, *49*
Smith, Will, 36
Staubach, Roger, 47
Street Justice (TV series), 35
Sudan, 20, 21

Tenochtitlan, 24
Texas, 5, *8*, 11, 12, 39, 41
Texas Western College (University of Texas-El Paso), 15
Tomás and the Library Lady (1989 book), 16
Treaty of Guadalupe-Hidalgo, 5
Treviño, Jesús Salvador, 52
Tufts University, 19

Valdez, Luis, 52
Vargaz, Jacob, *26*
Villar, Antonio Ramon Sr., 29
Villar, Natalia, 29
Villaraigosa, Antonio
    birth and childhood, 29–30, 53
    political career of, 30–33
    scandals involving, 31, 33
Villaraigosa, Corina, 29, 33

Ugly Betty (TV series), 37
Underwood, Carrie, 49
UNICEF, *37*
United Farm Workers, 9
United Nations, 17, 20
United States, 5, 6, 8, 9, 10, 11, 12, 13, 17, 18, 24, 29, 33, 34, 41, 50, 51
University of California at Los Angeles (UCLA), 25, 30
University of Texas, 15
Utah, 5

Walkout (2006 film), 27
Washington, D.C., 19
World War II, 8

ZZ Top, 41

PICTURE CREDITS

ABOUT THE AUTHOR

Hal Marcovitz is the author of more than 100 books for young readers. A former newspaper journalist, he makes his home in Chalfont, Pennsylvania.